Clean Your Heart
澈心明典

Clean Your Heart
澈心明典

Enlightenment Book 开悟之书

Jiang 作者江

PARTRIDGE

To order additional copies of this book, contact
Toll Free 800 101 2657 (Singapore)
Toll Free 1 800 81 7340 (Malaysia)
orders.singapore@partridgepublishing.com

www.partridgepublishing.com/singapore

Contents

Introduction

This book is intended to Enlighten people. Human consciousness is like a computer system, and the faith system is the foundation program for sustaining the whole system.

Truth is like a bug to smash all programs. When the bug makes the whole system break down, enlightenment is reached. There will be a non-system human.

When one person unloads the system, wisdom may appear.

If you require milk, you need a glass.

This system is a constraint. When people free themselves from it, they become who they naturally are. The process may be a little uncomfortable because people still think they are the system itself.

This book includes several courses which need to be copied by handwriting or typing. It doesn't matter whether people think or not; this material is processed in the subconscious.

Course 1

Are there really eyeballs? Why is it not the information from touch and images that returns to the brain and then is perceived? Why not? Why no?

Are there really noses? Why is it not the information from touch and images that returns to the brain and then is perceived? Why not? Why no?

Are there really mouths? Why is it not the information from touch and images that returns to the brain and then is perceived? Why not? Why no?

Are there really ears? Why is it not the information from touch, voice, and images that returns to the brain and then is perceived? Why not? Why no?

Are there really tongues? Why is it not the information from touch and images that returns to the brain and then is perceived? Why not? Why no?

You may use them every day, but do you know what they really are?

Stay piece and alone.

Course 2

Is anxiety real? Why is it not the information from scent, touch, voice, taste, and images that returns to the brain and then triggers the program in the brain, or it operates automatically, and then is perceived? Why not? Why no?

Is uneasy real? Why is it not the information from scent, touch, voice, taste, and images that returns to the brain and then triggers the program in the brain, or it operates automatically, and then is perceived? Why not? Why no?

Is fear real? Why is it not the information from scent, touch, voice, taste, and images that returns to the brain and then triggers the program in the brain, or it operates automatically, and then is perceived? Why not? Why no?

Is anger real? Why is it not the information from scent, touch, voice, taste, and images that returns to the brain and then triggers the program in the brain, or it operates automatically, and then is perceived? Why not? Why no?

Is pride real? Why is it not the information from scent, touch, voice, taste, and images that returns to the brain and then triggers the program

in the brain, or it operates automatically, and then is perceived? Why not? Why no?

Emotions are always taking control of us. What if they are just a collection of programs?

Course 3

Is the body real? Why is it not the information from scent, touch, voice, taste, and images that returns to the brain and then is perceived? Why not? Why no?

Is the brain real? Why is it not the information from scent, touch, voice, taste, and images that returns to the brain and then is perceived? Why not? Why no?

Am I real? Why is it not the information from scent, touch, voice, taste, and images that returns to the brain, creating various ideas, and then is perceived? Why not? Why no?

Is despair real? Why is it not the information from scent, touch, voice, taste, and images that returns to the brain and then triggers the program in the brain, or it operates automatically, and then is perceived? Why not? Why no?

Are friends real? Why is it not the information from scent, touch, voice, taste, and images that returns to the brain and then is perceived? Why not? Why no?

You can ask yourself similar questions.

Course 4

Is family real? Why is it not the information from scent, touch, voice, taste, and images that returns to the brain and then is perceived? Why not? Why no?

Is Buddha real? Why is it not the information from scent, touch, voice, and images that returns to the brain and then is perceived? Why not? Why no?

Is Jesus real? Why is it not the information from scent, touch, voice, taste, and images that returns to the brain and then is perceived? Why not? Why no?

Is Muhammad real? Why is it not the information of scent, touch, voice, taste, and images that returns to the brain and then is perceived? Why not? Why no?

Is God real? Why is it not the information from scent, touch, voice, taste, and images that returns to the brain and then is perceived? Why not? Why no?

Is Allah real? Why is it not the information from scent, touch, voice, taste, and images that returns to the brain and then is perceived? Why not? Why no?

Is Siva real? Why is it not the information from scent, touch, voice, taste, and images that returns to the brain and then is perceived? Why not? Why no?

Is Krishna real? Why is it not the information from scent, touch, voice, taste, and images that returns to the brain and then is perceived? Why not? Why no?

God is a source code, and the character system is the original sin. When the character system is unloaded, the spirit will go back to the source code.

Course 5

Is image real? Why is it not the information that returns to the brain and then is perceived? Why not? Why no?

Is voice real? Why is it not the information that returns to the brain and then is perceived? Why not? Why no?

Is touch real? Why is it not the information that returns to the brain and then is perceived? Why not? Why no?

Is scent real? Why is it not the information that returns to the brain and then is perceived? Why not? Why no?

Is gustation real? Why is it not the information that returns to the brain and then is perceived? Why not? Why no?

Use the program. See if you can acquire something beyond.

Course 6

Is belief real? Why is it not the information from scent, touch, voice, and images that returns to the brain and then triggers the program of the brain, or it operates automatically, and then is perceived? Why not? Why no?

Is doubt real? Why is it not the information from scent, touch, voice, taste, and images that returns to the brain and then triggers the program of the brain, or it operates automatically, and then is perceived? Why not? Why no?

Is judgement real? Why is it not the information from scent, touch, voice, taste, and images that returns to the brain and then triggers the program of the brain, or it operates automatically, and then is perceived? Why not? Why no?

Is vanity real? Why is it not the information from scent, touch, voice, taste, and images that returns to the brain and then triggers the program of the brain, or it operates automatically, and then is perceived? Why not? Why no?

Is attempt real? Why is it not the information from scent, touch, voice, taste, and images that returns to the brain and then triggers the program of the brain, or it operates automatically, and then is perceived? Why not? Why no?

Course 7

Is time real? Why is it not the information from scent, touch, voice, taste, and images that returns to the brain and then is perceived? Why not? Why no?

Is space real? Why is it not the information from scent, touch, voice, taste, and images that returns to the brain and then is perceived? Why not? Why no?

Is anger real? Why is it not the information from scent, touch, voice, taste, and images that returns to the brain and then triggers the program of the brain, or it operates automatically, and then is perceived? Why not? Why no?

Is thinking real? Why is it not the information from scent, touch, voice, taste, and images that returns to the brain and then triggers the program of the brain, or it operates automatically, and then is perceived? Why not? Why no?

Is calculation real? Why is it not the information from scent, touch, voice, taste, and images that returns to the brain and then triggers the program of the brain, or it operates automatically, and then is perceived? Why not? Why no?

Course 8

Is daze real? Why is it not the information of scent, touch, voice, taste, and images that returns to the brain and then triggers the program of the brain, or it operates automatically, and then is perceived? Why not? Why no?

Is idea real? Why is it not the information of scent, touch, voice, taste, and images that returns to the brain and then triggers the program of the brain, or it operates automatically, and then is perceived? Why not? Why no?

Is cognizing real? Why is it not the information of scent, touch, voice, taste, and images that returns to the brain and then triggers the program of the brain, or it operates automatically, and then is perceived? Why not? Why no?

Is karma real? Why is it not the information of scent, touch, voice, taste, and images that returns to the brain and then is perceived? Why not? Why no?

Is faith real? Why is it not the information of scent, touch, voice, taste, and images that returns to the brain and then triggers the program of the brain, or it operates automatically, and then is perceived? Why not? Why no?

Course 9

Is free will real? Why is it not the information of scent, touch, voice, taste, and images that returns to the brain and then triggers the program of the brain, or it operates automatically, and then is perceived? Why not? Why no?

Is joy real? Why is it not the information of scent, touch, voice, taste, and images that returns to the brain and then triggers the program of the brain, or it operates automatically, and then is perceived? Why not? Why no?

Is distinguishing real? Why is it not the information of scent, touch, voice, taste, and images that returns to the brain and then triggers the program of the brain, or it operates automatically, and then is perceived? Why not? Why no?

Is collective consciousness real? Why is it not the information of scent, touch, voice, taste, and images that returns to the brain and then is perceived? Why not? Why no?

Is material universe real? Why is it not the information of scent, touch, voice, taste, and images that returns to the brain and then is perceived? Why not? Why no?

Course 10

Is wisdom real? Why is it not the information of scent, touch, voice, taste, and images that returns to the brain and then triggers the program of the brain, or it operates automatically, and then is perceived? Why not? Why no?

Is freedom real? Why is it not the information of scent, touch, voice, taste, and images that returns to the brain and then is perceived? Why not? Why no?

Is evaluating real? Why is it not the information of scent, touch, voice, taste, and images which returns to the brain and then triggers the program of the brain, or it operates automatically, and then is perceived? Why not? Why no?

Is struggle real? Why is it not the information of scent, touch, voice, taste, and images that returns to the brain and then triggers the program of the brain, or it operates automatically, and then is perceived? Why not? Why no?

Is creating real? Why is it not the information of scent, touch, voice, taste, and images that returns to the brain and then triggers the program of the brain, or it operates automatically, and then is perceived? Why not? Why no?

Course 11

Is logic real? Why is it not the information of scent, touch, voice, taste, and images that returns to the brain and then triggers the program of the brain, or it operates automatically, and then is perceived? Why not? Why no?

Is value real? Why is it not the information of scent, touch, voice, taste, and images that returns to the brain and then is perceived? Why not? Why no?

Is envy real? Why is it not the information of scent, touch, voice, taste, and images that returns to the brain and then triggers the program of the brain, or it operates automatically, and then is perceived? Why not? Why no?

Is operation real? Why is it not the information of scent, touch, voice, taste, and images that returns to the brain and then triggers the program of the brain, or it operates automatically, and then is perceived? Why not? Why no?

Is irritation real? Why is it not the information of scent, touch, voice, taste, and images that returns to the brain and then triggers the program of the brain, or it operates automatically, and then is perceived? Why not? Why no?

Course 12

Is boredom real? Why is it not the information of scent, touch, voice, taste, and images that returns to the brain and then triggers the program of the brain, or it operates automatically, and then is perceived? Why not? Why no?

Is aspiration real? Why is it not the information of scent, touch, voice, taste, and images that returns to the brain and then triggers the program of the brain, or it operates automatically, and then is perceived? Why not? Why no?

Is desire real? Why is it not the information of scent, touch, voice, taste, and images that returns to the brain and then triggers the program of the brain, or it operates automatically, and then is perceived? Why not? Why no?

Is comparison real? Why is it not the information of scent, touch, voice, taste, and images that returns to the brain and then triggers the program of the brain, or it operates automatically, and then is perceived? Why not? Why no?

Is wish real? Why is it not the information of scent, touch, voice, taste, and images that returns to the brain and then triggers the program of the brain, or it operates automatically, and then is perceived? Why not? Why no?

Course 13

Is indifference real? Why is it not the information of scent, touch, voice, taste, and images that returns to the brain and then triggers the program of the brain, or it operates automatically, and then is perceived? Why not? Why no?

Is the outside world real? Why is it not the information of scent, touch, voice, taste, and images that returns to the brain and then is perceived? Why not? Why no?

Are others real? Why is it not the information of scent, touch, voice, taste, and images that returns to the brain and then is perceived? Why not? Why no?

Is pity real? Why is it not the information of scent, touch, voice, taste, and images that returns to the brain and then triggers the program of the brain, or it operates automatically, and then is perceived? Why not? Why no?

Is being thankful real? Why is it not the information of scent, touch, voice, taste, and images that returns to the brain and then triggers the program of the brain, or it operates automatically, and then is perceived? Why not? Why no?

Course 14

Is the past real? Why is it not the information of scent, touch, voice, taste, and images that returns to the brain and then is perceived? Why not? Why no?

Is now real? Why is it not the information of scent, touch, voice, taste, and images that returns to the brain and then is perceived? Why not? Why no?

Is the future real? Why is it not the information of scent, touch, voice, taste, and images that returns to the brain and then is perceived? Why not? Why no?

Is the desire to attack real? Why is it not the information of scent, touch, voice, sense of taste, and images that returns to the brain and then triggers the program of brain, or it operates automatically, and then is perceived? Why not? Why no?

Is desire to control real? Why is it not the information of scent, touch, voice, taste, and images that returns to the brain and then triggers the program of the brain, or it operates automatically, and then is perceived? Why not? Why no?

Course 15

Is repression real? Why is it not the information of scent, touch, voice, taste, and images that returns to the brain and then triggers the program of the brain, or it operates automatically, and then is perceived? Why not? Why no?

Is sense of honour real? Why is it not the information of scent, touch, voice, taste, and images that returns to the brain and then triggers the program of the brain, or it operates automatically, and then is perceived? Why not? Why no?

Is sense of safety real? Why is it not the information of scent, touch, voice, taste, and images that returns to the brain and then triggers the program of the brain, or it operates automatically, and then is perceived? Why not? Why no?

Is insistence real? Why is it not the information of scent, touch, voice, taste, and images that returns to the brain and then triggers the program of the brain, or it operates automatically, and then is perceived? Why not? Why no?

Is sense of worth real? Why is it not the information of scent, touch, voice, taste, and images that returns to the brain and then triggers the program of the brain, or it operates automatically, and then is perceived? Why not? Why no?

Course 16

Is peace real? Why is it not the information of scent, touch, voice, taste, and images that returns to the brain and then triggers the program of the brain, or it operates automatically, and then is perceived? Why not? Why no?

Is calm real? Why is it not the information of scent, touch, voice, taste, and images that returns to the brain and then triggers the program of the brain, or it operates automatically, and then is perceived? Why not? Why no?

Is inability real? Why is it not the information of scent, touch, voice, taste, and images that returns to the brain and then triggers the program of the brain, or it operates automatically, and then is perceived? Why not? Why no?

Is worry real? Why is it not the information of scent, touch, voice, taste, and images that returns to the brain and then triggers the program of the brain, or it operates automatically, and then is perceived? Why not? Why no?

Is mantra real? Why is it not the information of scent, touch, voice, taste, and images that returns to the brain and then is perceived? Why not? Why no?

Course 17

Is chaos real? Why is it not the information of scent, touch, voice, taste, and images that returns to the brain and then triggers the program of the brain, or it operates automatically, and then is perceived? Why not? Why no?

Is blocking real? Why is it not the information of scent, touch, voice, taste, and images that returns to the brain and then triggers the program of the brain, or it operates automatically, and then is perceived? Why not? Why no?

Is blame real? Why is it not the information of scent, touch, voice, taste, and images that returns to the brain and then triggers the program of the brain, or it operates automatically, and then is perceived? Why not? Why no?

Is sense of guilt real? Why is it not the information of scent, touch, voice, taste, and images that returns to the brain and then triggers the program of the brain, or it operates automatically, and then is perceived? Why not? Why no?

Is the environment real? Why is it not the information of scent, touch, voice, taste, and images that returns to the brain and then is perceived? Why not? Why no?

Course 18

Is lust real? Why is it not the information of scent, touch, voice, taste, and images that returns to the brain and then triggers the program of the brain, or it operates automatically, and then is perceived? Why not? Why no?

Is love real? Why is it not the information of scent, touch, voice, taste, and images that returns to the brain and then triggers the program of the brain, or it operates automatically, and then is perceived? Why not? Why no?

Is happiness real? Why is it not the information of scent, touch, voice, taste and images that returns to the brain and then triggers the program of the brain, or it operates automatically, and then is perceived? Why not? Why no?

Is sadness real? Why is it not the information of scent, touch, voice, taste, and images that returns to the brain and then triggers the program of the brain, or it operates automatically, and then is perceived? Why not? Why no?

Is beauty real? Why is it not the information of scent, touch, voice, taste, and images that returns to the brain and then is perceived? Why not? Why no?

Course 19

Is harmony real? Why is it not the information of scent, touch, voice, taste, and images that returns to the brain and then is perceived? Why not? Why no?

Is safeness real? Why is it not the information of scent, touch, voice, taste, and images that returns to the brain and then is perceived? Why not? Why no?

Is danger real? Why is it not the information of scent, touch, voice, taste, and images that returns to the brain and then is perceived? Why not? Why no?

Is acceptance real? Why is it not the information of scent, touch, voice, taste, and images that returns to the brain and then triggers the program of the brain, or it operates automatically, and then is perceived? Why not? Why no?

Is maintenance real? Why is it not the information of scent, touch, voice, taste, and images that returns to the brain and then triggers the program of the brain, or it operates automatically, and then is perceived? Why not? Why no?

Course 20

Is memory real? Why is it not the information of scent, touch, voice, taste, and images that returns to the brain and then triggers the program of the brain, or it operates automatically, and then is perceived? Why not? Why no?

Is forcing real? Why is it not the information of scent, touch, voice, taste, and images that returns to the brain and then triggers the program of the brain, or it operates automatically, and then is perceived? Why not? Why no?

Is there really a me? Why is it not the information of scent, touch, voice, taste, and images that returns to the brain and then its perceived? Why not? Why no?

Is bashfulness real? Why is it not the information of scent, touch, voice, taste, and images that returns to the brain and then triggers the program of the brain, or it operates automatically, and then is perceived? Why not? Why no?

Is caring real? Why is it not the information of scent, touch, voice, taste, and images that returns to the brain and then triggers the program of the brain, or it operates automatically, and then is perceived? Why not? Why no?

Course 21

Is frustration real? Why is it not the information of scent, touch, voice, taste, and images that returns to the brain and then triggers the program of the brain, or it operates automatically, and then is perceived? Why not? Why no?

Is distress real? Why is it not the information of scent, touch, voice, taste, and images that returns to the brain and then triggers the program of the brain, or it operates automatically, and then is perceived? Why not? Why no?

Is the sense of existence real? Why is it not the information of scent, touch, voice, taste, and images that returns to the brain and then triggers the program of the brain, or it operates automatically, and then is perceived? Why not? Why no?

Is premonition real? Why is it not the information of scent, touch, voice, taste, and images that returns to the brain and then triggers the program of the brain, or it operates automatically, and then is perceived? Why not? Why no?

Is respect real? Why is it not the information of scent, touch, voice, taste, and images that returns to the brain and then triggers the program of the brain, or it operates automatically, and then is perceived? Why not? Why no?

Course 22

Is comfort real? Why is it not the information of scent, touch, voice, taste, and images that returns to the brain and then triggers the program of the brain, or it operates automatically, and then is perceived? Why not? Why no?

Is terror real? Why is it not the information of scent, touch, voice, taste, and images that returns to the brain and then is perceived? Why not? Why no?

Is thirst real? Why is it not the information of scent, touch, voice, taste, and images that returns to the brain and then triggers the program of the brain, or it operates automatically, and then is perceived? Why not? Why no?

Is hunger real? Why is it not the information of scent, touch, voice, taste, and images that returns to the brain and then triggers the program of the brain, or it operates automatically, and then is perceived? Why not? Why no?

Is attention real? Why is it not the information of scent, touch, voice, taste, and images that returns to the brain and then triggers the program of the brain, or it operates automatically, and then is perceived? Why not? Why no?

Course 23

Is selfness real? Why is it not the information of scent, touch, voice, taste, and images that returns to the brain and then triggers the program of the brain, or it operates automatically, and then is perceived? Why not? Why no?

Is selfishness real? Why is it not the information of scent, touch, voice, taste, and images that returns to the brain and then triggers the program of the brain, or it operates automatically, and then is perceived? Why not? Why no?

Is selflessness real? Why is it not the information of scent, touch, voice, taste, and images that returns to the brain and then triggers the program of the brain, or it operates automatically, and then is perceived? Why not? Why no?

Is foolishness real? Why is it not the information of scent, touch, voice, taste, and images that returns to the brain and then triggers the program of the brain, or it operates automatically, and then is perceived? Why not? Why no?

Is clumsiness real? Why is it not the information of scent, touch, voice, taste, and images that returns to the brain and then triggers the program of the brain, or it operates automatically, and then is perceived? Why not? Why no?

Course 24

Is greed real? Why is it not the information of scent, touch, voice, taste, and images that returns to the brain and then triggers the program of the brain, or it operates automatically, and then is perceived? Why not? Why no?

Is sense of going fast real? Why is it not the information of scent, touch, voice, taste, and images that returns to the brain and then triggers the program of the brain, or it operates automatically, and then is perceived? Why not? Why no?

Is sense of going slow real? Why is it not the information of scent, touch, voice, taste, and images that returns to the brain and then triggers the program of the brain, or it operates automatically, and then is perceived? Why not? Why no?

Is differentiation real? Why is it not the information of scent, touch, voice, taste, and images that returns to the brain and then triggers the program of the brain, or it operates automatically, and then is perceived? Why not? Why no?

Is indolence real? Why is it not the information of scent, touch, voice, taste, and images that returns to the brain and then triggers the program of the brain, or it operates automatically, and then is perceived? Why not? Why no?

Course 25

Is comprehension real? Why is it not the information of scent, touch, voice, taste, and images that returns to the brain and then triggers the program of the brain, or it operates automatically, and then is perceived? Why not? Why no?

Is addiction real? Why is it not the information of scent, touch, voice, taste, and images that returns to the brain and then triggers the program of the brain, or it operates automatically, and then is perceived? Why not? Why no?

Is obsession real? Why is it not the information of scent, touch, voice, taste, and images that returns to the brain and then triggers the program of the brain, or it operates automatically, and then is perceived? Why not? Why no?

Is persecution real? Why is it not the information of scent, touch, voice, taste, and images that returns to the brain and then is perceived? Why not? Why no?

Is awakening real? Why is it not the information of scent, touch, voice, taste, and images that returns to the brain and then triggers the program of the brain, or it operates automatically, and then is perceived? Why not? Why no?

Course 26

Is enlightenment real? Why is it not the information of scent, touch, voice, taste, and images that returns to the brain and then triggers the program of the brain, or it operates automatically, and then is perceived? Why not? Why no?

Is vacancy real? Why is it not the information of scent, touch, voice, taste, and images that returns to the brain and then triggers the program of the brain, or it operates automatically, and then is perceived? Why not? Why no?

Is positivity real? Why is it not the information of scent, touch, voice, taste, and images that returns to the brain and then triggers the program of the brain, or it operates automatically, and then is perceived? Why not? Why no?

Is negativity real? Why is it not the information of scent, touch, voice, taste, and images that returns to the brain and then triggers the program of the brain, or it operates automatically, and then is perceived? Why not? Why no?

Is anxiety real? Why is it not the information of scent, touch, voice, taste, and images that returns to the brain and then triggers the program of the brain, or it operates automatically, and then is perceived? Why not? Why no?

Course 27

Is fluster real? Why is it not the information of scent, touch, voice, taste, and images that returns to the brain and then triggers the program of the brain, or it operates automatically, and then is perceived? Why not? Why no?

Is forwardness real? Why is it not the information of scent, touch, voice, taste, and images that returns to the brain and then triggers the program of the brain, or it operates automatically, and then is perceived? Why not? Why no?

Is separation real? Why is it not the information of scent, touch, voice, taste, and images that returns to the brain and then is perceived? Why not? Why no?

Is encounter real? Why is it not the information of scent, touch, voice, taste, and images that returns to the brain and then is perceived? Why not? Why no?

Is courage real? Why is it not the information of scent, touch, voice, taste, and images that returns to the brain and then triggers the program of the brain, or it operates automatically, and then is perceived? Why not? Why no?

Is confusion real? Why is it not the information of scent, touch, voice, taste, and images that returns to the brain and then triggers the program of the brain, or it operates automatically, and then is perceived? Why not? Why no?

Are these courses real? Why is it not the information of scent, touch, voice, taste, and images that returns to the brain and then is perceived? Why not? Why no?

Is truth real? Why is it not the information of scent, touch, voice, taste, and images that returns to the brain and then is perceived? Why not? Why no?

Printed in the United States
By Bookmasters